BLOOD MAKES ME FAINT BUT I GO FOR IT

Natalie Lyalin

Ugly Duckling Presse 2014

Blood Makes Me Faint but I Go for It
© 2014 by Natalie Lyalin

ISBN 978-1-937027-33-9

Distributed to the trade by
Small Press Distribution
spdbooks.org

Eastern European Poets Series #34
First Edition, First Printing
1000 copies

Ugly Duckling Presse
The Old American Can Factory
232 Third Street #E-303
Brooklyn, NY 11215

Designed by Action at a Distance
Cover Illustration by Christopher Russell
Typeset in Myriad and Nanum Myeongjo/Gothic
Cover stock by French Paper

Printed and bound by McNaughton & Gunn

This publication was made possible in part by generous grants
from the National Endowment for the Arts and the New York State
Council on the Arts.

CONTENTS

For my parents.

One, two, three, four sacred tremors
A drop, they forgot the drop of blood!
What made them forget
They haven't forgotten

—Dmitri A. Prigov, *Fifty Drops of Blood*

First Husband

I stayed in the kitchen
I stayed with my knives
and my spoons and their meanings
In the morning I turned down the heat
Despite winter, I did not wear socks
I stepped into dead grass
and combed my hair back severely
I was exhausted and mean
He was close by and very eerie
He did not do the dishes
He retreated into our house
or he rode away in cabs
He rode far away from me
Of the two lakes he chose the closest
He threw things out of windows
my handmade things (mostly)
In the morning I pretended to sleep
but I saw his wings extend slightly
and his mellow form leaping out our dirty window

Mild Stigmata

I did not panic over my stigmata. It was mild!
It was a tiny welt on each hand, and another
on my right ankle. There was no blood!
We looked at it together, my husband and I.
Lover, I said. I'm the chosen one, I said.
He did not get it. He did not get my disease.
The stigmata drove him out. And still, I did not panic.
I will not panic, I said. This is a faith crisis. This is
a chance for some good counseling. The stigmata
stayed. I poured it a bath. Was this Jesus coming
out? I told him to stay hidden. Was this a new
and fabulous leprosy? No, it was a freakin'
sign! It was a sign of things to come! Decent,
honest things, in this newest year of our Lord.

Small and Private Tragedies

The cow was cold and yet I milked it. Under a dirty blanket I found something warm, so I held it tightly. It was my own hand, don't worry. Under a slanted sky I cursed the cold and kept on going. My mountain is called grief I say, and when feeling toothed, that is, when teeth come into a conversation I miss mine. I also miss my father and mother being married, because that was when we did all this terrible work together. Now this frost reflects my wounded mouth to me and in the shower, under very hot water, I cackle at the thought of things past. I make a bird call and confuse the others. I set the clocks back. My insanity is precious. It is a gem I smuggled out and now it is a moon over this fortress.

Agrarian

In a photograph I kiss a horse and look foreign
A goat dies
Something changes in my eyes and I am terrifying
A light comes on or goes off
Blood makes me faint but I still go for it
Blindly, I hoof it around the barn kicking at things
That pig diseased me, I think
A darkness comes and goes without settling
Today the moon was a black circle in a mud sky
Tomorrow the sun will blind me
In a fugue state I lick my fur parts clean and roost
Hello, I am a new type of animal
There are gaggles of us out in the country
We are singing in our mother tongues
Our mother's tongues, we are using them
Sometimes I say my name is Kelly from Ohio
Sometimes I am more mythical
I am a great angry thing with thick feathers
I am hiding rings in my rose-stank mouth

Over Yonder

In my collapsed summer home
behind my bigger summer home
I experience sunburn
I dream of a submarine in hostile waters
I take a turn into being American
See, I am so American with my hopes
I make tapestries and ask, "Is this dumb? Is this dumb?"
I weave a forest in the south
The whole family looking on
A heavy summer sleep
while waiting for the guillotine
Before the body turned
before I hated animals
I stretched out in a hammock and shared diseases
My head in an ache from all the life I was in

Black Horse Pike

I took my wagon onto Black Horse Pike
Without blankets!
With plenty of water
With a real tiredness!
Without regret
With throbbing paws!
Without thinking
With questions!
Without direction
With my ghostly sons!
Without my daughter
With my mother's anger!
Without her rifle
With a target on my back!
Without worry
With letters and numbers!
Without a message
With a sense of exploration!
Without much concern for others
With a sense of ownership!
Without a contract
With a vague promise of justice!
Without juice
With a faulty eye socket!

Without a correction
With a small erection!
Without a wedding veil
With a bothersome tooth!
Without a way to fix it
With an arrow!
Without a weapon
With a navigator!
Without common sense
With my dear friend!
As skulls lit the road
As wheat braided itself into circles
As hawks predicted our end

Pale Orange Safari

Is this an illness?
This is an illness imagined
I imagined landing in an airport and feeling dizzy
Dizziness, a sign of something terrible, surely!
I remembered the first tornado after father left home
I felt very angry later, but first, panicked
I helped mother stash the jewelry

A storm tore though the proud south
Even later, family money sent me to Europe
I swear it was nice that no one met me in the airport
That is how I preferred it!

Pale White Irises

I had no desire for work but work found me
I depended on certain forces to move me along
Now parts of me did not want to move
I was afraid of contracting dementia
Mental illness never scared me until I really thought about it
And everyone else seemed to have talent
Marjorie was good at art
Fatima was a baseball player
I just had these irises and their mournful stalks
And spring was unsettling
Terrible jokes leapt out of me
The sun had many knives of light

Stalingrad, 1943

There was a squawk sound and the clouds flipped to green, the sky, yellow. I was counting seeds and noted the moment. It was a strange farm, a strange town, a frightened country we were in. There were not too many schools or children, so there were few balloons. I concerned myself with the sickly garden. It needed bone meal so I got some. Under the moon's coloring thirty foxes circled my house and sixty wolves circled them. I called my grandmother to say that I would name someone Wolf, and she thought this splendid. We hung up, but I told her to keep living. Keep living though you are very far away from your country, and your friends are not coming home. Bad things happened, but I harvested a giant pepper and ate it whole. And it was very hot and also splendid. I spied a rake and began a short-lived revolution.

I Love Those Stags

I mounted the fake stag
This one had necklaces hanging on his antlers
I predicted he could actually hear me
I was tired
See, I had been blanching and icing all day
Also making delicately fried chicken
I provided cloth napkins for everyone
They all came over and we drank
Some said this was a happy moment
Some promised to never return
I mounted a cold, fake animal in the night
The highway glittered out like real America racing in circles
Why, why, why, did they all not go home?
I provided chicken, napkins, opportunity—all of these things
Still, those crazy, cold stags refused to leave
With a tender stomachache I pretended to dry heave into a bucket
This sent them galloping into the uncertain night

Oregon Is All Water

The death canoe contrasts the quiet lakes. You are smothering me. Literally, with a pillow. I spent last night choking you. Before that you hid in the closet with a small axe. You chopped at me. I attacked you with a hammer. You blasted back with a homemade firebomb. I scalped you old-school style. You snuck up with a lethal punch to the temple. Oregon is unfolding all around. The monster trees, who knows what they are hiding. What crazy beasts live in the solid woods? This is the place of deep vacation. We are moving closer to insane nature. It is moving through us. I'm plowing this land down to the bone, to the place where stench comes from. Verdant and cataclysmic. I'm in the place of small plane crashes and hatchets. I'm pretty sure we are going to battle back out of this place.

I Want to Lead All These Lives

Someone is always screeching. In the distance husbands bring home orange flowers. There is orange-flavored Ceylon and a mysterious powder and the metal oven door. In this silence I made up things to say and then felt better. The things I let float away into the past. I'm still thinking of you. I still love you. Hysteria is funny. It produces mountains that float by. Snow clings to the ground somewhere. Droughts happen. Nothing we have done really makes sense. Also, the most accurate memories are ones we never access. I've accessed all of mine and hacked them. I was the ice queen in first grade. I was the balloon released a year earlier. I'm an electrical engineer. I was robbed in a stairwell. My gold teeth were pulled out. I suffered greatly and am still suffering. I keep having heart attacks out in the open. And it is not safe there, in front of all those people. I slapped my hand away from my own chocolate cake. I scared myself in the dark and turned myself over and over. I said, let me take you to the Promised Land, I rode a chariot, I grew a giant beard. It took me months to trace myself back to myself. I'm my own father and mother and all the geese that ever flew past your wide-open windows.

Resuscitations

What began in a cave is
still happening indoors
That's where the plants are
in my archive
Of tragedies
mixed with gladiolas
and other life mulched into soil
You see, I am repulsed by weakness
In photographs I am stumbling
up the stairs
This is raw
A whole bar of raw
I am not afraid of the ocean
I am not afraid of work
Pop a bottle top
without a corkscrew
Use a sword!
The American Heritage Dictionary contains a flaming sun
Onions float in outer space
Radishes are a part of earth
Every morning I do not swoon
but swoosh down a chimney just for fun
And there are bones around my cauldron
but they do not mean much

I am a myth, like
if Jesus had a wife
she would be beautiful
I want to eat the other half
of the melon
Not your head, fish head
Not your cloves
Not your sacred bits stored up for winter
Winter, that is what I am waiting for
Without ambition or a direction
like ghosts that make a compass spin
Something about magnetic energy
and how there are black holes to
disappear into
Overnight, the world shrinks
I escape
but I don't escape all the way
Today is Yom Kippur
I am full of chocolate
What happens in a desert does not matter
Actually, it does
I have a hairpin in my mouth
A neighbor lights a sparkler
And it's like a night in East Jerusalem

The good kind
I love you
and all the gates
In a previous life
I was Joseph Stalin's personal secretary
He liked telling us what to do
and we would murmur
Joseph, Joseph
do not be so angry
Your portraits are still hanging
in all of our living rooms

Your Brain Is Yours

I am baptized by coins with a faint smell of elderflower
I transfigure, blink in one part of the house and then another
A holy night unfolds and stands weakly
A child chemist mixes a star in a test tube
Glass shatters lightly
I am a saint
I soothe with marmalade and tonic
I embroider a pillow and give it a squeeze
I attach a heavy gold necklace to a horse rump
We clang along across the empire
Every church window flies open in greeting
Every bell rings weary
I stretch my arms out and receive light
My face appears on a tree
Red flowers spring forward
I attend a funeral, and then another
My face appears in water, lightly distorted
I am tired like the ancients were tired

Saturday

The more terrible things in the world sat by the window
They undulated, smoking away in wisps
I stepped out to toss some water
The neighbor, with his tongue out, wore a necklace of heads
The flowers bloomed early
I swiped the curtains closed
My heart stopped but did not blow up
It remained suspended, a weird meaty flower
surrounded by ribs that resemble tusks

You Should See My White Vest

My dad said it looks like a woven cloud
and my mother laughed and laughed
Your father is a lamp! Is a table!
He is under a curse
He is secretly leaving the country
and we must intercept him
before he throws paint on the Vatican's ceiling
before he rips off the Pope's rings
He should see my sloppy garden
my hot soup
He should see the way I drift in the house
smoke in my ears
a sugar cube in my mouth
How I poison myself with dove meat
He should see my doves
their enormous cages in my house
on top of the house
a large, yellow parrot in my basement
He should see my projects
My origami fortress
My other origami fortress

I Should Not Be Afraid

I am all sugar skulls and guns
The fog around the mountain reassures me
It hides good and evil things from the world
That means someone in the universe is thinking
That means there is an equation about the future
I will not understand it
I will leave it out in the open
You can find it in my dream home next to the clawfoot tub
You will solve it while looking out a window
And I will be an atom
I will help the sugar woman of Oaxaca make skulls
Some as small as quarters
Others as large as real human ones

Future Weather

In the future someone always loses. The arsonist killed
it last night! We slept by the front door and listened.
I warmed my hands by the light of fire and waited.
Huge ugly satellites flew over us constantly. They were
predicting our downfall. They were collecting some
information. My neighbor slinked around in my housecoat.
I was the weird person to be friends with. Do not fear me,
small angry children. I was once just like you!

On the Beaches of Majorca

Aboard ships they snapped goodbye to their cities
They sparkled like knives
And the oceans took them in with oceanic slurps
In a parallel moment we were on the beaches
Mute pastel puffs
Smoking around a cult-like fire
We sent our loves away and waited for correspondence
We read tea leaves and cards
We graffitied the names of saints
We slumped over to concerts and danced in a daze
This was the year no one remembers
No one recalls the sagging stands in the market full of apples and scarves
Though we ate the apples
and wrapped our heads in the scarves
Anticipated news of what our lives would be like
Would we be widows
or continue to give off weak, colored light?

A Fever Was Coming

The whales carried a sickness
We swam through them, unnoticed
Untouched, we passed their tails
And behind the water
a God of seasons
One who observes the harvest
One who chimes bells
Today we had a visitor
It was your father
He was angry
He insisted on things that could not happen
He rattled
A pen burst
Our water acquired an acrid taste
We took the boats out
We were unlicensed
We would not harpoon
We would feel our bodies
They would be ours only
Other people were only hours old
They were enlightened and shiny
The water kept unfolding
We sailed into a bloody sunset
A banged up dusk

The Occidental Mountains

This is a dispatch:

Douglas-fir, Apache Pine, Chihuahua Pine, Mexican Pinyon Pine, Lumholtz's Pine, Yecora Pine, Rocky Mountain Douglas-fir, and Mexican Douglas-fir.

Arizona White Oak, Emory Oak, Mexican Blue Oak. Large skinny hawks overhead.

This is a love letter:

A lot of people are going to have a good time at your expense. It is your turn to put on a party. You all should carry buckets together. No, you all should tip a cow together. No, you all should bale hay together. We are no longer on the mountain.

This is a pre-nup:

For every year you stay in the mountains they owe you something. Come on, mountains. At least attend my great aunt's funeral. I could cling to you. You could hold me with your pines and oaks. For every year you are married to the mountains they owe you a new car. For every child you have with the mountain you get an Appaloosa. The mountain and you will have adult relations at least once a week, for every week, not counting holidays. Should the mountains be unfaithful you can level them with some very large hammers.

This is a rice scroll:

The mountains are hiding older mountains. They are sinking back into the ground. Some mountains are known for fossils. Others are bear-hiders. The mountains will sometimes ask you to leave things behind. For example, your arm. You do not need that one arm. Please, give it to the mountains. Or they will ask for it with their voices, which have not been heard for eons, and are probably very dangerous to the mental health of humanity.

Zusya, Open Your Ears

You are in the cosmos with Dora and Raisa,
Sophia, Wolf, Ansa, and Rivka

You are all circling, circling
You are all drinking tea, having a good laugh!

Zusya, I call out to you in your earthly namelessness
In a small hole, I invent you from nothing

Zusya, you are faceless
Some cells pulling in different directions

Zusya, this is a resurrection

You are now an algorithm
or a piece of gristle in a wet mouth
or a hen's white egg

Zusya, your bones
your fear, once real, now nothing

Zusya is the sound of a tuning fork, an alien hum in the water
A jellyfish, electrifying a black sea,
or a rock formation,
or a tree

The New New Testament

You came down a mountain with a grass tuft
You, you, you, left your county of origin
Your private pig
You became mythic
A mist overtaking the lowlands
The badlands, the country houses with curtains
You, a pine baron
A possessor of trees
You, you, you, went out for milk in Alabama
You scuttled aboard a boat
You found a gold arrowhead
And now?
Now? Now? Now?
You are probably a baby in India
You are probably happy
Are you sending us signals?
Are you sending us signals in the form of scents?
We are ridiculous
And you
you, you, you
are a kayak
You are red
And you are water in our buckets
And you are fire in our stoves

And you, you, you, are molecules

All knowing and understanding

You are in a pasture

There are no shadows

You are bigger than everything

You are very small

You are my camp mate

I row you out to the middle of the lake

I tell you some mean things

And you

you, you, you

You wave me off

You are an eucalyptus branch

You are blonde and foreign

In The Future We Are Not Screaming

We are singing
and our songs are not evil
They do not reach the sailors
The icebergs in the dark
A sea with random fireworks
A rose that burrows the night
We are a myth but not that type of myth
We are holy the way Boris and Gleb were holy
So we take shape in our father's hearts
They see our saintliness
They darken our streets and hang up a rainbow
Our neighborhoods look weak
Our skin turns, goes from glow to glowing
Somehow it is all assassinate! Assassinate!
In the morning the smell outside is wooden, woods, woody
Wood curls blowing through the street
In the future we are all forgiving
We succumb to pleats
We forgive the tight braids our mothers gave us
We make phone calls—
Surprise!

I was in your kitchen and drilled through a pipe
I kissed your brother's lips
therefore I am unsettled
There are no horses here
Our voices are weird in these tabernacles

Burn, Burn, Burn the Air

I lined up my geese and sent them flying.
Into a hot night I dribbled rounded pearlies off of lips.
Upside down glass domes contracted, as if living.
As if living was your choice anyway. Anyway, we went
walking. The galaxies tried to part us. We were then
pardoned for the war crimes. It was only after that we
lead them to the mass graves. With some gravitas we
dug for survivors. There were none, so they hanged us!
They hanged us in the brightest spot of our youth. Before
that we took guns and tried to stop them. There were many
invasions and they all came with chants.

Electrocardiogram

I protect my heart when I perform, but the night is another thing
It does not appear to care much, and I am weak
Nightmare: my father is a bride. I lift the veil over his eager face
His wife's eyes are very dark suckling holes
I fasten some pearls around his neck and send him off
Grow well, little dad! Send me a postcard when you wake up
I will have you over for a nice lunch
We will make a toast with your new champagne glasses!
They will sizzle and froth over with our clinks

Tell Them What I Used to Be

On stage in Hamburg in all my glitter
Tell them how I refused things
How much caviar I ate
How I ran a factory
Extracted spoons from stomachs
All those small things
Tell them how I was ugly
Tell them how hot am I right now
How my brain is encased in lucite
and cut into sections
Tell them my right eye is an enormous diamond
How my hands are preserved white and bone-like
Tell them about the milk I milked and from which animal
and how I restrained that animal to get it
How I starved in a forest and how my fear left me
Tell them how I marched for hours on my hands
Through the snow, through a tundra
How the animals howled and how I responded with a whistle
An Arctic tune I inherited from my peoples

There Is Milk in Them Hills

I went to find your father
Because I saw his spirit
Because I saw his spirit chasing moccasins from our front door
Because I saw his shadow
Because I saw him throw a shadow on our nettles

I went to them hills and they were clambering
chugging out some rote sounds
So I halved a rock and joined them
and in a cave I found him, molting

He was becoming something tangible
All muscle and yellow bone
A skin coming in on the edges
We heard grass growing
Heard the pinecones making spheres
So we yipped ourselves to a silence and waited
So we went iris to iris
So we did not touch because he was still delicate

Then he picked a tough skin
and it reverberated
scrambling our grids and what not

And let it be known that he came with no memory
How he appeared in the night airs!
And how those airs soothed him!

In our hills, in this nowhere county

Was That Not You

Was that not you in the milkweeds?
In some photographs you are smoking, playing chess, wearing flattened hats

Guess what, we are selling your suits

Was that you in the forest?
You with timber?
There are all these stories of you in Siberia
Wrestling tigers
Solving some equation

In the summers you picked wild berries
You closed a knife on your fingers
Your tonsils had to be taken out

Now we've let some animals inside
So you cannot return
I'm saying to you, this is over
Do not cry and make hand gestures like the shotgun

International Women's Day

On this day we got carnations and balloons

I ate a lobster-shaped lollipop that tasted like death
In ballet class I floundered with a stomach cramp
I danced like an injury dancing
There were swimming lessons in the hospital's pool
There were chess lessons in the room next to it
I lied about my birthday and the chess students clapped
In an etiquette class I bloodied a pretty nose
My teacher wore her red bikini out into snow
We ate bread and sugar
This was before we let go of the furniture

This was after the hospital

This was before the difficult things started

It was the first difficult thing

Be Still, Pine

Wind, slice the grain open
Tractor, work the stooped land
Practice plane, fly lower
Katarina, scrub the floors
Holeb, build an oven
Marina, solve the equation
Josef, climb into Holeb's oven
Wind, scatter Josef's ashes
Katarina, kiss Marina
Marina, make a pipe bomb
Josef, resurrect thyself
Tractor, keep going
Practice plane, start landing
Katarina, get to the control tower
Holeb, assume a dive position
Marina, send in the others
Josef, stop your crying
Practice plane, please take them
Marina, cut all their hair off
Wind, bring this hair to the birdies
Tractor, run them over
Holeb, this is your time
Marina, this is your time
Josef, this is your time
Katarina, this is your time

The House Was So Alone

The rooms were slick with griefs

My rocking horse moved unassisted

In a parallel universe my aunt planted seeds outside

Planted them all over the soils

Back in real time we sat around waiting

We joined a cult

It was beautiful

Our cult, it was helpful to others

We were not phantoms

No, we were real gems

We had depth

But our house

It remained a mystery

Who survived there?

Who survived?

There were rules for us

They stretched out in silver bands

On our mouths, that is where we put them

Things were illegal, were delicious

This is what they dared us to do

Drink your Kool-Aid

Drink all your drinks

Have a roast in the backyard

the way they do it in Hawaii

We wore white
This meant something
And, who survived it?
Who made it out?
We wore white
and it meant nothing
They tried to take us in vans
and we said no
We stayed on
By then it was all facts and figures
numbers and odds
What did it mean?
The worst happened
I found myself tired
but I found myself

Bulgarian Cough Remedy

The cure involves onions
A catholic desire to enter the woods
at night
under the yellow moon

cataracted by the mist always lifting off the ground

Bulgaria, where all of our grandfathers are from
Your crest is in our collective cells
Your cells smelling of lakes
On your shores we probably emerged from the water
dumbstruck by all the green oxygen clinging over everything

Your rivers are the Iskar, Struma, and Maritsa
and I'm sure it means something
that your people know how to help the lungs
How to recover the memories
of summers on the Iskar
diving in to touch the black rocks

Forgive the gross inaccuracies as you come
to us as a vision, holy-like, an ornate
tapestry of fur and gold thread
depicting a Jesus hanging out under some breasts

As a whole, your children are young-looking
and many are twins, tentatively holding up the peace sign
in photographs with drying garlic in the background

Release the Teeth

Your mother is ill
I send her letters dipped in goldleaf
That is the color of the real leaves pierced by a sun
Today this sun is ferocious
My mother keeps me from the beach
My phone is old and seven years ago it rang
Today we learned about bacteria and how it is important
My jaw is wired and restrung
You put ice cubes in your mouth
We collect rainwater for our baths
Our baths are grand
Akin to a resurrection

And here I am in my pastels

Here I go with my arms out

I Had This Hair When My Dad Was Alive

I'm from a sturgeon's lung
I'm cut out and breathing
The weather is changing languages
All over, the equinox is taking away power
Different weird clouds keep forming
Darling things come in twos!
We are both alive and in Poland
Foreign foghorns keep sounding
In your city the police are absolutely corrupted
Farm animals are finally getting to eat succulent grasses
The invisible typewriter is suspended in space
This hair is authentic fox fur
Coffins are so tiny after dark!
Toxic sludge has made its way into the heartland!
Under a heavy rain we keep walking
Everyone is sharing photos of their babies
The waiter will not bring me juice
I keep stopping by weird French restaurants
The car lost a wheel just as I pulled up
The first snow fell and I'm angry!
This man is having a seizure on the elliptical
My family is incognito
Twenty-eight years ago things were so different!
It was hard to find boots and stockings

In the cover of night men are sneaking into windows
Parking lots are full of unwanted baggage
We found galoshes and rubber diapers
Your new friends are much better than me
All over the world people are being birthed
Our grandmothers can no longer see too far!
She's exaggerating her stupid pain
The proboscis stunned me into silence
We thought your name would be Vladimir
My television is resting on a teeny tiny stand
This music is from Swan Lake!
My mucus is coming up yellow
The outdoor patio is really a lanai
The youngest child is always the prettiest
This wedding is full of cancer-causing sugar!
In a past life I was someone really crazy
This old old country is the grave's keeper!
The steroids are starting to wear off
This trench coat smells of urine
I've shopped with your baby!
The raccoon traps are howling

Red Currant / Black Currant

My mother hurries a dress across the ocean, like I am a wild
boar bride tearing open for a big gown. Chasms are blooming.
It is time to unfreeze the meals and heat the home.

But I want to go back in time and not be so terrible.
I could give warning: things do not end well.

So now there are articles about the near extinct penguin
and polar bear. There are grainy shots of the Tasmanian tiger
pacing behind a fence. Perhaps I should go warn him instead.

Look, the birds are flying in a V formation, headed right into
our fireworks. Right into our celebratory rum and punch,
and our carved pineapple.

Let us never make photos of this or our wedding, or our birth,
or anything that happens after or before. Photos are small reminders
of how we cannot time travel. We cannot go back to warn or forward
to see how it all turned out.

Drank a Pine Tree

In a week you can so love someone
Take them to the woods
Wrap them in a fur cloak
Point out tremendous lichen
Singe a steak bone

Then move into the woods
This is an experiment
Like a sugared nut that settles the stomach
Like how the planets are confused

This is why a dull tuft of grass greeted us this morning
This is why the doctor saw a sickly robin

The world is ending in preparation for a new one

The dumbest luxury we invented were cruise ships
and drinks of electric colors
I am sure of this
Like how God is on a mountain
on all the mountains at once
How he hides from us
because we are terrible

Like how we say, this book is for you
and for you, and for you
but it is for no one in particular

A Lemon Sweat Over Everything

You can find my bones in the sister mountains
Identify me by the gold fangs
The fangs I showed you in the lemon orchard
almost two hundred years ago
You said they were sexy
The sun blinding you from my mouth
We were both smirking
and then I snarled
It was very foreign
chasing you around the trees

Sun Bone

My love is in a hovercraft
in a vessel ringed with diamonds
My love sheaths her arrows
in a gelatinous ocean
My love levitates the trees
of minor mountains
My love bleaches bones
under all three suns
My love braids the grass
around a grave stone
My love uses magnets
but not in the normal way
My love shelters thieves
but only the good ones
My love drinks air through a straw
but not all the air, and not all at once
My love travels in a schooner
but without irony
My love reinvented the wheel
and it looks softer
My love flies to another country
but she will not tell me which country
or what language they speak
or what I should send her

The Guillotine Comes Down Like This

I spent the summer watching over mother
bobbing on the ocean
Grandfather's new girlfriend was gentle
under our umbrella

What did we send off into the sky?

An azure balloon

Marisa's hair ribbon

I sent off a wisp of hair into the Atlantic

My heart got hard, less fragile
We invented a poison for our parents
They laughed it away, jumped overboard
I liked everything about our neighbor
I liked the white hydrangeas best

How I tried to drown myself!
All cut up with gold flecks
translucent stone and spittle
and a spill
A block of zebrawood
buoyant

Holy Animals

Believe me, the animals are holy
George from Georgia is fixing my locks, refusing tea

And now, now, is the right time

God's wing descends from the sky and covers my mouth

I hold up my house as a peace offering
Do not smite us today for we already feel smote
Let us sleep on the grass all winter long
In the summer, give us watermelons
Let my small-headed animal grow a spike, a poisonous horn
then she will not be so fragile

George built us a fine lock but we have no curtains
The house is bright with the Lord's promise that glows our foreheads
We warm milk
There is no evil
There is not a darkness on our roof
Our grandmothers tried to protect us with salt and spittle
This almost always worked

Buckshot

This is the last time I write about birds. Birds, who cares about your wings? Who admires your feathers? Who keeps you from entering my windows? I do. Birds, with your distinct calls, and your disregard for my birthday, and your nests all around. Where were you when my salad sucked? Where were you when I headed out of town? You have let me down.

For the hunt I take hats. My rubber boots, too. I eat flapjacks in the smoky haze of my pipes, my corncob pipes. I clean guns and check things. I hunt in the night, like a blind alligator, like a stunned mouse.

Goodbye, all you sounds, all you flaps, all you guns. Goodbye to my deer stand, glowing in the light of the things I have done.

That Milk

Good milk gives away nothing
It sits in supreme judgment of us
and I'm trying to be a better person
but it is hard
Oren, I am attempting things
Mostly hallucinating
I thought your folded-up coat was a cake
The chair a pausing giraffe
My anger a type of fossil that requires a hammer
My hammer a type of tool that is made of porcelain
See how I get it all wrong
I called Seth to complain and have not stopped
I called dad to check on him and it got weird
We were talking about the eyes and how losing one is not so bad
But I was wrong, it would be horrible
I thought the prism was a walrus
and the table another cake
and the dirty plate a spaceship with no doors
It was just like the movies but totally different
It was like life but totally funny
It was like giving birth on a spaceship
or to a spaceship
It was weird
like I'm wired wrong

I hate you and your light fixtures
And your parties, non-stop
Your non-stick pans arranged in some deranged order
I don't see it
I am sorry

I am still working
on my mural of Louisiana
I'm drawing it on a tile
free-hand, so it is terrible
But I gloss over the devastation
which is amazing

I am rewriting all of our histories
We are on a show together
We are okay
In my version of the story I am the big sweaty king
and my husband is the blond princess resting on my chest

I do not wake us
There is no need
We have a fire

Thank you to the generous editors of *6x6*, *Supermachine*, *Denver Quarterly*, *Octopus Magazine*, *The Offending Adam*, *Jellyroll Magazine*, *Sixth Finch*, *Bone Bouquet Journal*, *"Poem-a-Day"* from the Academy of American Poets, *Jubilat*, *Elective Affinities*, *Two Serious Ladies*, *Storyscape Literary Journal*, *notnostrums*, *Rowboatcop*, and *Weird Deer* for first publishing these poems.

A small portion of this book was first published as the chapbook *Try A Little Time Travel* (Ugly Duckling Presse, 2010).

Special thanks to Seth Landman for reading and re-reading the manuscript that is now this book.

With love, for Vade Bolton, who is here and everywhere all at once.